Toward an Angola Strategy: Prioritizing U.S.-Angola Relations

Toward an Angola Strategy: Prioritizing U.S.-Angola Relations

An Independent Commission Report

Sponsored by the Council on Foreign Relations
The Center for Preventive Action

Founded in 1921, the Council on Foreign on Foreign Relations is an independent, national membership organization and a nonpartisan center for scholars dedicated to producing and disseminating ideas so that individual and corporate members, as well as policymakers, journalists, students, and interested citizens in the United States and other countries, can better understand the world and the foreign policy choices facing the United States and other governments. The Council does this by convening meetings; conducting a wide-ranging Studies program; publishing *Foreign Affairs*, the preeminent journal covering international affairs and U.S. foreign policy; maintaining a diverse membership; sponsoring Independent Task Forces; and providing up-to-date information about the world and U.S. foreign policy on the Council's website, CFR.org.

THE COUNCIL TAKES NO INSTITUTIONAL POSITION ON POLICY ISSUES AND HAS NO AFFILIATION WITH THE U.S. GOVERNMENT. ALL STATEMENTS OF FACT AND EXPRESSIONS OF OPINION CONTAINED IN ALL ITS PUBLICA-TIONS ARE THE SOLE RESPONSIBILITY OF THE AUTHOR OR AUTHORS.

The Council will sponsor an Independent Commission when (1) an issue of current and critical importance to U.S. foreign policy arises, and (2) it seems that a group diverse in backgrounds and perspectives may, nonetheless, be able to reach a meaningful consensus on a policy through private and nonpartisan deliberations. Typically, a commission meets between two and five times over a brief period to ensure the relevance of its work.

Upon reaching a conclusion, a commission issues a report, and the Council publishes its text and posts it on the Council website. commission reports can take three forms: (1) a strong and meaningful policy consensus, with commission members endorsing the general policy thrust and judgments reached by the group, though not necessarily every finding and recommen-dation; (2) a report stating the various policy positions, each as sharply and fairly as possible; or (3) a "Chairman's Report," where commission members who agree with the chairman's report may associate themselves with it, while those who disagree may submit dissenting statements. Upon reaching a conclusion, a commission may also ask individuals who were not members of the commission to associate themselves with the commission report to enhance its impact. All commission reports "benchmark" their findings against current administration policy in order to make explicit areas of agreement and disagreement. The commission is solely responsible for its report. The Council takes no institutional position.

For further information about the Council or this commission report, please write the Council on Foreign Relations, 58 East 68th Street, New York, NY 10021, or call the Director of Communications at 212-434-9400. Visit our website, CFR.org.

Commission Chairs

Vincent A. Mai

Frank G. Wisner

Project Director

William L. Nash

Deputy Project Director

Adam P. Frankel

Commission Members

Contents

Foreword   xi

Acknowledgments   xiii

Maps   xvi

List of Acronyms   xviii

Commission Report   1

    Executive Summary   3

    Introduction: Why Angola?   8

    A Nation in Transition   10

    Postwar Challenges   16

    Rethinking U.S. Strategy toward Angola   30

    U.S. Policy Recommendations   40

    Conclusion   45

Commission Members   49

CPA Mission Statement   57

CPA Advisory Committee   59

Foreword

Peace has become a reality in Angola since the end of its bloody, twenty-seven-year civil war in 2002. However, much work remains to be done if Angola is to become a democratic state with an inclusive and prosperous society. It is in the interest of the United States to help develop a sustainable and lasting peace in Angola—not only for the security of U.S. energy supplies, but also to promote stability in southern Africa. In so doing, the United States must tread carefully, because while Angola's leaders respect and, at heart, want a strong relationship with the United States, there are many in Angola who—based in part on the history of U.S.-Angola relations—are suspicious of American policy.

The mission of the Council's Center for Preventive Action (CPA) is to help prevent, defuse, or resolve conflicts in countries or regions that may otherwise be overlooked. After a careful assessment of the country, the CPA's Independent Preventive Action Commission finds Angola to be an emerging power on the African continent, one with the potential to realize long-term stability and prosperity. Sensitive that any proposals must not exceed the reach of American power and influence—and recognizing that stamping out corruption or producing respect for democracy in a manner Americans would recognize, especially after centuries of Portuguese colonial rule in the country and decades of civil war, is a long-term goal—the commission aimed to be realistic in its recommendations. The commission believes that the United States should firmly and clearly state that nurturing U.S.-Angola relations is important to the United States. In addition to increased diplomatic attention and sustained assistance, the United States can take steps to advance shared objectives through more regular bilateral discussions, cooperation with multilateral organizations, and innovative partnerships with private enterprises.

The Council and the CPA are indebted to Vincent A. Mai and Frank G. Wisner, the commission's cochairs, for their leadership and perseverance in this effort to study U.S.-Angola relations and delineate a strategic vision for U.S. policy toward Angola. Along with the cochairs, twenty commissioners—including distinguished scholars, former U.S. government officials, international organization officials, and leaders of business and nongovernmental organizations—devoted nearly two years of effort to this project. Princeton N. Lyman deserves thanks for his extraordinary guidance on all things Africa and his tireless efforts to broaden the basis for U.S. engagement on the continent.

Finally, I wish to thank CPA Director and General John W. Vessey Senior Fellow for Conflict Prevention William L. Nash for his management of the project. Throughout the work of the commission, Bill kept the project's broadest goals in mind: promoting development, good governance, and reconciliation in countries that have moved beyond conflict so that the conditions that threaten stability do not reassert themselves.

Richard N. Haass
President
Council on Foreign Relations
April 2007

Acknowledgments

First and foremost, I would like to thank commission cochairs Vincent Mai and Frank Wisner for their time and energy throughout the duration of this project. Their wisdom, keen instincts, and collegial work style not only made the report possible, but gave it authority and significance.

We had a very talented and experienced group of commissioners, including two former U.S. assistant secretaries of state and a host of seasoned diplomats and international organization officials, Africa experts, businesspeople, and nongovernment leaders. All of their advice, detailed attention to multiple report drafts, and patience was essential and greatly appreciated. The expertise of Princeton N. Lyman, director of the Council's Africa Policy Studies program during most of the commission's work, was invaluable. Edward V.K. "Kim" Jaycox, a commission member, stepped in for other commissioners and led the research delegation to Angola. When flights were cancelled, he never skipped a beat. Adam Frankel then took the commission's ideas and crafted the foundation for the report.

Angola's Ambassador to the United States Josefina Pitra Diakite graciously met with the commission and helped the commission prepare for travel to Angola. U.S. Ambassador to Angola Cynthia G. Efird welcomed our effort and her embassy team helped us arrange meetings during our trip to the country.

We are also grateful to all those who helped us in Angola but who for various reasons remain anonymous.

The commission is grateful to Richard N. Haass and Gary Samore for supporting an effort about an often overlooked—yet strategically important—country, and for providing invaluable comments on the report's substance. Their hard questions served to sharpen our focus.

On behalf of the chairs and myself, I want to thank Jamie Ekern, the research associate at the Center for Preventive Action for her tireless efforts. Her intellect, drive, and thoroughness were crucial for the completion of this report.

We at the Center for Preventive Action are sincerely thankful to Patrick M. Byrne and his family for generously supporting the General John W. Vessey Senior Fellow for Conflict Prevention. John G. Heimann, Swanee Hunt, James D. Zirin, and John W. Vessey himself continue to give important support to the center. In addition, we are grateful to the Carnegie Corporation of New York whose grant made this project possible.

Finally, I would note that this report was finalized in mid-March 2007. Our report takes into account developments in Angola and U.S.-Angola relations up to that point.

William L. Nash
Project Director

Gulf of Guinea Region

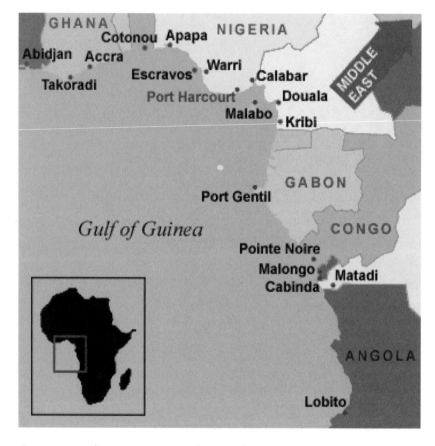

Angola

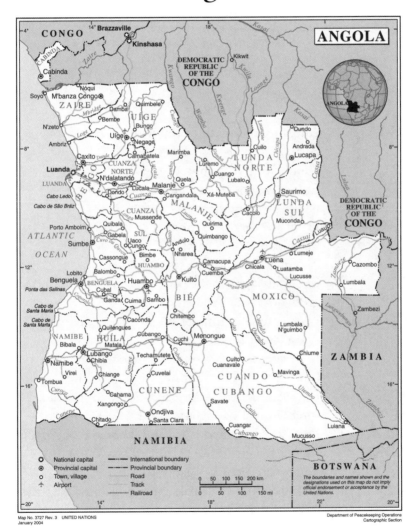

Map No. 3727 Rev. 3   UNITED NATIONS
January 2004

Department of Peacekeeping Operations
Cartographic Section

Source: www.un.org/Depts/Cartographic/map/profile/angola.pdf.

Acronyms

AGOA	African Growth and Opportunity Act
AU	African Union
DRC	Democratic Republic of the Congo
EITI	Extractive Industries Transparency Initiative
FAA	Angolan Armed Forces
FLEC	Front for the Liberation of the Enclave of Cabinda
FNLA	National Liberation Front of Angola
FTA	free trade agreement
GDP	gross domestic product
ICITAP	International Criminal Investigative Training Assistance Program
IDA	International Development Association
ILEA	International Law Enforcement Academy
IMET	International Military Education and Training
IMF	International Monetary Fund
MPLA	Popular Movement for the Liberation of Angola
NEPAD	New Partnership for Africa's Development
NGO	nongovernmental organization
OPEC	Organization of Petroleum Exporting Countries
PSI	Policy Support Instrument
SADC	Southern African Development Community
TIFA	Trade and Investment Framework Agreement
UNDP	United Nations Development Programme

| UNITA | National Union for the Total Independence of Angola |
| USAID | U.S. Agency for International Development |

Commission Report

Executive Summary

Outside the continent's crisis areas, few African countries are more important to U.S. interests than Angola. The second-largest oil producer in Africa, Angola's success or failure in transitioning from nearly thirty years of war toward peace and democracy has implications for the stability of the U.S. oil supply as well as the stability of central and southern Africa. Consequently, the United States has an interest in helping Angola address its numerous and significant national challenges.

At the same time, the United States would not be true to its tradition of democratic values if it did not express concern about the development of democratic governance, protection of human rights, and the rule of law in Angola. Much progress has been made in public transparency and tolerance of dissent, but there is still a way to go. Angola's great wealth is still held by few, and the country continues to rank poorly in terms of human development and governance. Furthermore, an immense amount of physical reconstruction and psychological rehabilitation remains to be done. Angola must wisely use the wealth created by its abundance of natural resources by investing in education, training, and institutional capacity building. It will take years of commitment and determination for Angola to prove to its own people, its neighbors, and the world that it can meet the goals it has set for itself.

Given that U.S. policy toward Angola is a difficult issue for policymakers, businesspeople, and civil society, building a stronger relationship with Luanda will be the most effective means for the United States to help Angola make progress toward peace, democracy, and equitable

3

development, while simultaneously looking after U.S. interests in the Gulf of Guinea region. As part of the U.S. efforts to develop both a broad energy policy and a strategic approach toward Africa, Angola deserves much greater attention in the formulation of U.S. foreign, national security, and economic policies.

Adopting a strategic vision for relations with Angola and strengthening U.S.-Angola relations requires sustained U.S. diplomatic attention and strategic resource allocation. It also involves building trust and strong lines of communication. To begin, the United States can associate itself with sensible Angolan priorities, take steps to advance shared, nonpolitical objectives, and commence regular bilateral discussions with a comprehensive agenda. Common objectives, such as education, public health, poverty alleviation, and institutional capacity building, should be advanced through bilateral assistance and support for international organizations.

An integral part of this policy must also be for the United States, working in partnership with international and regional organizations like the United Nations (UN), World Bank, and African Union (AU), to support those individuals in Angola—political leaders, community activists, and civil society leaders—who are striving to build from within a democratic country in which good governance and a more equitable distribution of national wealth are regarded as national priorities. This can be done without undermining the development of a stronger bilateral partnership between the United States and Angola.

The United States must also develop a multilateral strategy to advance the goals of regional security, stability, and development. The Southern African Development Community's (SADC) SADC-U.S. Forum is one setting in which to discuss the political and security situation in the region, and to evaluate progress in areas of cooperation. It is important that the United States support and coordinate with international institutions, both behind the scenes and publicly, to help Angola achieve its development goals and build the infrastructure and human capacity it needs for sustained growth.

Greater levels of U.S. private sector investment in Angola depend more on action by the Angolan government than by the U.S. government. Investment will increase when the Angolan government takes steps to make its business climate more user-friendly and its overall economy less dependent on oil. That said, by sponsoring trade and investment missions, U.S. government departments can help fill information gaps for financiers and businesspeople in a range of sectors, perhaps ultimately building bridges to Angolan businesses and expanding commercial ties.

So deep and complex are Angola's problems, and so sensitive is the history of U.S.-Angola relations, that relatively modest goals must be set for the near and medium term and then achieved only incrementally. Without foregoing commitments to promoting democratic governance and the rule of law, the United States must show patience and forbearance—rebuilding a country after so much destruction, and creating a more equitable society in which Angola's leaders are politically accountable, will not be achieved quickly. Yet sustained attention is the best way to develop long-term partners who contribute to international stability and the best conflict-prevention strategy available.

To that end, the commission recommends:

Bilateral

- The Bush administration launch a series of visits by congressional delegations and high-level administration officials, such as the undersecretary of state for economic affairs, to southern African states, including Angola, that are making progress in democratic and economic development.

- The assistant secretary of state for African affairs visit Luanda to discuss Angola's national elections, capacity needs, and postconflict reconstruction and reconciliation process, as well as to compare assessments about developments in the Democratic Republic of Congo (DRC) and Zimbabwe.

- The U.S. Department of State facilitate a discussion with the Angolan government and representatives from the U.S. private sector, nonprofit community, and higher education institutions to explore the possibility of public-private partnerships in capacity building and technical assistance.

- The U.S. government maintain the approximately $35 million of U.S. bilateral assistance to Angolan institutions currently anticipated for 2008. Such funds should continue to provide technical assistance for democratic institution building, civil society, education and professional training, financial and land reform, agricultural development, and public health. Specifically, the Department of State's nonproliferation, antiterrorism, de-mining, and related programs funding, which supports the development of Angola's de-mining capability and the management and destruction of small arms, should not fall below the current $6 million for the next five years. Funding for International Military Education and Training (IMET) programs aimed at developing apolitical and transparent defense institutions, such as training in civil-military relations, defense budgeting, and human rights, should be increased to $600,000 annually.

- The U.S. Embassy discuss with Angola the possibility of expanding current law enforcement training programs with the International Law Enforcement Academy (ILEA) and establishing police institutional development programs through the International Criminal Investigation Training Assistance Program (ICITAP). Programming should include community policing, election security and civil disturbance techniques, and academy development.

- The U.S. Department of Defense make building rapport with Angola a priority of the new U.S. Africa Command. Increased engagement with the Angolan Armed Forces (FAA), through contacts and briefings with FAA leadership, should focus on the progress of disarmament, demobilization, and reintegration of former combatants, developments in the DRC and Zimbabwe, and the role of the FAA in postconflict Angola. Furthermore, the Department's Africa Center for Strategic Studies initiative can hold some of its leadership and topical seminars in Angola.

Multilateral

- The United States propose holding a SADC-U.S. Forum summit meeting in Luanda.

- The United States support an international investment and economic development conference for Angola, as recommended by the official representatives of donor countries in Luanda. This conference would be an opportunity for Angolan government and development stakeholders to discuss how to strengthen partnerships, prioritize development goals, and build the capacity Angola needs for sustained growth.

- The United States prepare to offer a technical assistance package that complements future cooperation between Angola and the International Monetary Fund (IMF).

Private Sector

- The United States articulate a free trade agreement (FTA) as a goal toward which the U.S. and Angolan governments can aspire, and set milestones for its completion, including an agreement on a Trade and Investment Framework Agreement (TIFA) to establish a consultative mechanism between the U.S. Trade Representative and the Angolan government.

- The United States continue the current practice of supplementing the funding for bilateral assistance programs by public-private agreements with private enterprises active in Angola.

- The U.S. Department of Commerce launch trade and investment missions, particularly for agricultural and agribusiness companies, and establish a permanent presence in the U.S. mission in Angola.

- American businesses operating in Angola, particularly oil companies, expand support for Angolan education institutions and support more advanced education and training opportunities for Angolan students.

Introduction: Why Angola?

The national challenges Angola faces are significant. Although Angola achieved independence in 1975, in a way it is only five years old, becoming whole only when its bloody civil war ended in 2002. Since then, the nation has embarked on a long, tough journey to become a more stable country, one that offers a "pole of stability" in Africa. To complete this transition successfully, Angola must rebuild its physical infrastructure, create democratic government institutions capable of providing public services, address the issues of transparency that have plagued its governance, reduce poverty and unemployment, develop its human capacity through education and training, revive its non-oil sectors, promote national reconciliation, and cultivate constructive international relationships—all of which could transform Angola into a more equitable society and prevent future instability. But while it holds the prospect of success, Angola's future is still uncertain. It will take years of commitment and determination for Angola to prove to its own people, its neighbors, and the world that it can meet the goals it has set for itself.

For these reasons the Council on Foreign Relations convened this Preventive Action Commission on Angola. After deliberation on the state of Angola's postconflict transition and the substance of U.S.-Angola relations, this commission believes that Angola deserves much greater attention in the formulation of U.S. foreign, national security, and economic policies, particularly as the United States seeks to develop a comprehensive policy toward Africa. The United States' relationship with Angola should receive significant diplomatic consideration and resources in recognition of its rising importance. U.S. interests in both a secure energy supply and stability in the Gulf of Guinea region require no less.

At the same time, this commission expressed concern about the development of democratic governance, protection of human rights, and adherence to the rule of law in Angola. Much progress has been made in public transparency and tolerance of dissent, but there is still a way to go. The same is true of democratic practice, particularly regarding elections. It is in the U.S. interest to discuss these concerns with Angolan leaders. At the same time, as Angola seeks to build productive political and economic partnerships, it is in Angola's interest to place all issues on the agenda. Comprehensive bilateral dialogue will be the most effective means to help Angola make progress toward peace, democracy, and equitable development.

Building sustained success and stability in Angola, however, is not a job for the Angolan and the U.S. governments alone. It is critical that the United States support institutions like the AU that are working throughout the continent, including in Angola, to promote democratic practice and human rights. It also requires that the United States consult with Angola's other partners, especially China, and collaborate with international organizations. Businesses and nongovernmental organizations (NGOs) also have important roles to play as Angola seeks to build its infrastructure and human capacity.

One final point is worth noting. Angola is one of several countries worldwide that are important suppliers of energy to the United States but face serious challenges with governance, equitable development, and human rights. Therefore, the recommendations in this report for forging deeper U.S.-Angola cooperation to advance mutual interests may have broader relevance. It is this commission's hope that the Angola strategy articulated in this report will help guide policymakers as they manage similarly complex relationships in Africa, Latin America, Central Asia, and elsewhere.

A Nation in Transition

With roughly thirteen million people in a territory nearly twice the size of Texas, Angola is blessed with a bounty of natural resources: offshore oil, coastal fisheries, mineral deposits, and fertile farmland. But Angola has a tragic past—a harrowing colonial heritage and an even more traumatic decolonization experience. Nearly five centuries of colonial rule, two decades of struggle for independence, and three decades of civil war took a toll on Angola, scarring the nation with massive loss of life and physical destruction. Angola today is a product of this cruel history. The wars' devastation provides an important, but incomplete, explanation for the pace of peacetime progress. No sensible U.S. policy can be designed without explicit recognition of Angola's destructive history and the difficulties facing the postwar Angolan state.

Historical Background

Angola's troubled relationships with Western powers began in the late fifteenth century when Portuguese ships docked along its shores. Soon after the Portuguese completed their military conquest of the Congo and Ndongo states, they began shipping Angolans and other Africans to the Americas. By the nineteenth century, Angola was a major source of slaves sent to Latin America, the Caribbean, and the United States. Angola was also very profitable for Portugal in other ways. By the mid-twentieth century, Angola was the fourth-largest coffee and sixth-largest diamond producer in the world, as well as the third-largest oil producer in sub-Saharan Africa.

But colonialism did not benefit most native Angolans. The Portuguese divided natives between *assimilados*, legal Portuguese citizens, and the rest—about 90 percent of the population—were subject to forced labor. Forced labor was used not only to extract agricultural and mineral resources, but also to construct three railroads from the Atlantic coast to the interior. One of these, the transcontinental Benguela railroad, linked the port of Lobito with the copper zones of the Belgian Congo, passing through what is now Zambia, to Dar es Salaam, Tanzania. The Portuguese regime also encouraged white immigration to Angola, especially after 1950, intensifying racial antagonisms and sowing the seeds of revolution among the black majority.

In the 1950s and 1960s, as other European powers shed colonial possessions in the face of growing support for independence, Portugal held fast to Angola. In response, three major independence movements with roots in different geographic and ethnic areas emerged. The Popular Movement for the Liberation of Angola (MPLA), led by Agostinho Neto, developed a following among the Mbundu people, the predominant ethnic group both in the region surrounding Luanda and in the Bengo, Cuanza Norte, Cuanza Sul, and Malanje provinces. This Marxist-oriented movement also included whites, *mestiços* (of mixed race), and Angola's urban and intellectual elites. The National Liberation Front of Angola (FNLA), led by Holden Roberto, represented the Bakongo ethnic group of northwestern and northern Angola. The National Union for the Total Independence of Angola (UNITA) was led by Jonas Savimbi and represented the largest ethnic group in Angola, the Ovimbundu of the central highlands and southern provinces. Colonial war consumed the country until a 1974 coup d'état in Portugal resulted in the installation of a more liberal military government determined to unburden itself of overseas colonies. Lisbon ended the war in Angola and agreed, in the Alvor Accords of January 1975, to hand over power to a coalition transitional government.

The agreement, however, rapidly fell apart due to power struggles among the three armed camps. With control of Luanda, the MPLA declared Angolan independence on November 11, 1975, as the Portuguese abandoned the capital. Agostinho Neto became the first president of the MPLA government. In response, UNITA and the FNLA formed a rival coalition government based in the interior city of Huambo, and fought against the MPLA for control of Angola. To finance operations for nearly three decades, the MPLA drew upon the revenues generated by offshore oil and the increasingly lucrative oil fields in the northern province of Cabinda. After the decline of the FNLA, UNITA continued to fight the government, financing its activities with funds accumulated by trading alluvial diamonds, mined in Angola's northeastern provinces.

The conflict among Angolan nationalist movements was exacerbated by their ties to larger powers in the global Cold War. The MPLA government was bolstered by Soviet military equipment and Cuban combat troops; UNITA—and for a time, the FNLA—received Chinese military equipments, U.S. military assistance, and South African military assistance and combat support.

By late 1987, with a thaw developing between the United States and the Soviet Union, national and international actors in Angola became increasingly responsive to the possibility of a negotiated settlement. After negotiations in London, Brazzaville, and Geneva, interlocking agreements, mediated by the United States in 1988, led to the withdrawal of Cuban and South African forces from Angola—a withdrawal monitored by the United Nations.

Despite these agreements, civil war persisted between the MPLA government and UNITA. U.S., Portuguese, and Russian mediation efforts to achieve power sharing culminated in the Bicesse Accords of 1991. This agreement attempted to institute a multiparty government in Angola, calling for UN-monitored democratic elections in 1992. However, when Jonas Savimbi of UNITA lost in the first round of voting, he declared the elections a fraud and led his troops back to war. UNITA had occupied nearly 70 percent of the country before the MPLA government, with new armaments and operational and training assistance from a private South African security firm, regained ground and brought Savimbi back to the negotiating table.

When UNITA failed to implement provisions of another national peace agreement, the Lusaka Protocol of 1994, the UN Security Council voted to impose sanctions against UNITA, dealing Savimbi a severe blow. He was forced to abandon his headquarters the following year, putting him on the run in eastern Angola. Seven years later, Savimbi was killed in a battle with Angolan government troops in Moxico province, paving the way for peace.

In April 2002, the MPLA and UNITA accepted a cease-fire in a memorandum of understanding, and later that year they agreed to resolve outstanding issues, such as the demobilization of UNITA, through the Lusaka Protocol. UN sanctions on UNITA were lifted on December 9, 2002. José Eduardo dos Santos, who came to power through internal party elections following President Neto's death in 1979, remains president to this day.

Ultimately, up to 1.5 million people—nearly 10 percent of Angola's total population—may have perished from 1975 to 2002. Approximately one hundred thousand Angolans were maimed by land mines, leaving Angola with the highest number of amputees per capita of any country in the world. International humanitarian organizations estimate that five hundred thousand Angolans fled into neighboring countries and over four million were internally displaced during the twenty-seven years of fighting.

Promise and Uncertainty

In many ways, Angola is a very different place today than it was just a few years ago. It has made progress in demobilizing combatants, managing the return of internally displaced persons and refugees, incorporating UNITA into the government, and building government institutions. In January 2007, Angola formally joined the Organization of Petroleum Exporting Countries (OPEC), underlining its growing role in the global energy system. The combination of record-high oil prices, increased oil production, and Chinese loans have jump-started Angola's development. In addition, a diverse group of foreign and Angolan actors—including political figures, civil society groups, diplomatic missions, international organizations, oil companies, international consulting firms, and bank executives—have all expressed cautious optimism that Angola is heading in the right direction regarding transparency and democratization.[1] For example, the Angolan government has signed

---

[1] This finding is based on Commission interviews in Luanda, June 24–28, 2006.

onto the UN Convention against Corruption and is updating the Ministry of Finance website regularly. In cooperation with the World Bank, Angola has established a program enabling government expenditures to be monitored in real time. International organizations operating in Angola note that civil society groups and opposition media are tolerated in Luanda, where one-third of the population lives, even though Radio Ecclesia, a notable opposition radio station, is not permitted to broadcast in the provinces.

However, even with these positive developments and the significant resources available to Angolan leaders to reinforce these trends, Angola faces a long, difficult road ahead. Angola is ranked 161 of 177 countries on the UN Development Programme's (UNDP) 2006 Human Development Index. Most Angolans struggle just to get through each day, with two-thirds of the population living in poverty on less than $2 per day.[2] Survival itself is a challenge—the average life expectancy is forty-seven years, more than 30 percent lower than the average for developing nations. Infant mortality and other measures of quality of life are among the worst in the world.[3] Concerning governance, Transparency International's 2006 Corruption Perceptions Index ranked Angola 142 out of 163 states. Ranking lower than it did the previous year, Angola was thirty-seven out of sixty countries—the "in-danger" risk category—on *Foreign Policy* and the Fund for Peace's 2006 Failed States Index. Angola has also earned a low standing in World Bank assessments on adherence to the rule of law. It will take years of commitment and determination by Angolan leaders both to ensure that the basic needs of average Angolans are met and to build a democratic society where power and wealth are shared more equitably.

While Angola's leaders seek recognition for what has been—and might still be—accomplished, they do not deny that much work remains. In fact, they are often frank about their country's challenges.

---

[2] The U.S. Central Intelligence Agency estimates that 70 percent of Angola's population lived in poverty in 2003. The UN Food and Agriculture Organization estimates that 40 percent of Angolans are undernourished, http://www.fao.org/faostat/foodsecurity/Countries/EN/Angola_e.pdf.

[3] World Bank, *Angola at a Glance*, August 24, 2005, http://devdata.worldbank.org/AAG/ago aag.pdf; Population Reference Bureau, *2005 World Population Data Sheet,* http://www.prb.org/pdf05/05WorldDataSheet_Eng.pdf.

Accordingly, the Angolan government has focused almost exclusively on domestic reconstruction since the end of the war, and has been highly selective about projecting influence abroad—with several notable exceptions. Although earlier it had intervened militarily in the DRC, Angola has more recently played a critical role in supporting the DRC peace processes, providing support to Congolese President Joseph Kabila. Angola is involved in the New Partnership for Africa's Development (NEPAD), a pan-African initiative to improve good governance and promote development. But while there is currently a mismatch between its growing strength and its involvement abroad, Angola is expected to play a larger role on the continent in the coming years, particularly once it strengthens its relationship with the SADC.

Angola has reached a crossroad. This moment represents a rare opportunity for Luanda to consolidate its peace and gain international standing. As a result of high oil prices, Angola has one of the fastest-growing economies in the world, enabling the government to invest in equitable development should it choose to do so. With smart investments in airports and seaports, Angola could serve the region as a transport hub. With investment in non-oil sectors, Angola could develop a diverse economy, better protected from the volatility of the oil market. By showing a strong commitment to the rule of law and transparency, Angolan leaders can encourage international investment and provide a model for other transitioning states. In the coming years, as Angola's leaders make decisions that will have lasting consequences for Angola and its neighbors, the world will be watching closely.

Postwar Challenges

The widespread destruction of Angolan territory during nearly three decades of civil war largely ruined Angola's economy, with one significant exception. Because much of Angola's oil is offshore, the oil industry was relatively undamaged during the war. With record-high international oil prices, the Angolan government's revenues skyrocketed. But without an experienced civil service translating that wealth into state services and jobs, national reconstruction has been astoundingly difficult.

The Economy

At the macroeconomic level, Angola is booming. Angola's gross domestic product (GDP) was $17.3 billion in 2004 and an estimated $24.3 billion in 2005. The IMF predicts real GDP growth of 14.3 percent for 2006 and 31.4 percent for 2007, putting Angola in the running for the fastest-growing economy in the world.[4] The fuel for Angola's economic engine is, of course, petroleum. The oil sector accounts for over 50 percent of Angola's gross national product, 95 percent of its exports, and 80 percent of Angolan government revenues.[5] Despite the ongoing smuggling of diamonds abroad, a large percentage of Angola's reported non-oil exports and revenue comes from the diamond industry. The mining sector has considerable untapped potential and is projected to show strong growth.

---

[4] IMF, "Regional Economic Outlook: Sub-Saharan Africa," September 2006, p. 40.
[5] U.S. Department of State, "Background Note: Angola," last updated March 2007.

Informal trade has also increased, with markets and vendors lining the streets in larger numbers, and economic activity beginning to spread beyond the capital. Luanda hopes the reopening of the entire Benguela rail line, expected in 2007, will revive the economy of the central highland region centered in Huambo.

In addition, inflation has declined significantly in recent years, falling from more than 300 percent to about 110 percent in 2001. Inflation declined further to 18.5 percent in 2005, and the government has set 10 percent as the target for 2006.[6] Reducing inflation from triple digits to double digits in just a few years is a remarkable achievement.

Angola's commercial banking sector has exploded—at least partly to meet the needs of Angola's elite. In addition to a growth in bank assets, the proportion of deposits that are lent as credit increased from 30 percent to 70 percent from 2002 to 2005.[7] As a result, Portuguese and South African banks are planning to open offices in Angola. In fact, Angola now represents over a quarter of net profits for the Portuguese Banco BPI.[8] Some Western analysts interpret this growth as a sign that banks are "betting on Angola."

It is critical for Angola to use the revenues generated by its nonrenewable resources to create jobs, services, and economic expansion for future generations. Ensuring that a buildup of foreign reserves does not lead to inflation, that wealth is spent wisely and managed transparently, and that domestic producers in non-oil sectors have an opportunity to grow, all require complex and sophisticated policies. Angola can gain valuable insights from the IMF and the World Bank on how to manage such issues.

While economic diversification could reduce Angola's vulnerability to fluctuations in the petroleum market and the potential consequences of large inflows of foreign currency from oil sales (also known as "Dutch disease"), foreign direct investment has yet to support a variety of

---

[6] IMF, "Angola: 2006 Article IV Consultations Preliminary Conclusions of the IMF Mission," March 29, 2006, conclusion No. 3, http://www.imf.org/external/np/ms/2006/032906.htm.

[7] U.S. Department of State, "2005 Investment Climate Statement—Angola," http://www.state.gov/e/eeb/ifd/2005/43019.htm.

[8] "Portugal PM Heads to Booming Angola to Boost Economic Ties," Agence France Presse, April 3, 2006.

economic sectors.[9] Investment remains weak outside the oil sector and industries involved in rebuilding Angola's infrastructure. Agriculture, once vibrant, has suffered the most. Prior to independence, Angola was the world's fourth-largest coffee exporter and one of the largest staple food exporters in sub-Saharan Africa. But during the war, when rural Angolans flocked to the coastal cities (mainly Luanda) for safety and work, fields and equipment were neglected or destroyed. Angola now imports approximately half of its food supply. To facilitate significant commercial agricultural development, recent land reform laws attempt to reconcile overlapping traditional land-use rights, colonial-era land claims, and modern land grants. Today, the agricultural sector is showing the first signs of sustained growth.[10] Reviving this industry, with its huge farming and fishing potential, could create jobs and help build a middle class—provided that the land does not become concentrated in the hands of a relatively small number of owners.

The Investment Climate

Angola's colonial heritage, pattern of development, and violent past have not left it well-placed to take maximum advantage of its wealth. Moreover, the impact of Angola's newfound prosperity is not widespread because the increased capital resources have not been channeled effectively into productive public and private sector investments. Angola's leaders assert their interest in private investment, but they have yet to make their country sufficiently open, in the view of many investors. Cronyism and the labyrinthine bureaucracy that businesses must navigate to turn a profit frighten away all but the most courageous investors. Angola is among the most difficult places in the world to do business. More than most countries, Angola strictly regulates business start-up

---

[9] Dutch disease is a term that broadly refers to the potential harmful consequences of large increases in a country's income. Although the "disease" is generally associated with a natural resource discovery, it can occur from any development that results in a large inflow of foreign currency, including a sharp surge in natural resource prices, foreign assistance, or foreign direct investment.

[10] IMF, "Angola: 2006 Article IV Consultations Preliminary Conclusions of the IMF Mission," conclusion No. 3.

and employment, although there has been some relaxation of employment rules in the past year. Property registration is difficult, and contract enforcement is inefficient. Overall, Angola ranks 156 out of 175 states in the Ease of Doing Business ranking, far behind many of its neighbors in Africa, according to *Doing Business 2007: How to Reform.*[11]

The business climate has improved moderately since the war ended in 2002. New legislation has been enacted both to provide incentives for private investment and to facilitate the establishment of commercial entities in Angola; the National Agency for Private Investment and the Guichet Único have been established as "one-stop shops" for fast-tracking business development.[12] The government is hoping that these measures will foster small-business growth, reduce the difficulty of doing business in Angola, and increase the confidence of potential investors.

Much more will need to be done to make Angola more attractive to foreign and domestic investors. With an increasingly integrated global economy, investors have a variety of choices about where to invest, and Angola is often seen as a place to avoid. Many financiers in the United States and around the world will not invest until Angola's business climate improves—both in absolute terms and relative to its neighbors. That said, Asian, European, and Latin American investors have fewer qualms than Americans about investing in Angola, and many are doing well.

In the end, improving the investment climate is the key to unlocking long-term growth and prosperity. Only an improved investment climate will attract the small businesses and foreign investment that can create new jobs and help build a viable middle class. A country where only a small group reaps the fruits of success will never have the market size or human capital it needs to build lasting private wealth.

Transparency

In recent years, high-level corruption has evolved—or devolved—into cronyism, with foreign investors required to collaborate with politically

---

[11] World Bank/International Finance Corporation, *Doing Business 2007: How to Reform,* http://www.doingbusiness.org/documents/DoingBusiness2007_Overview.pdf.

[12] This legislation includes Lei do Investimento Privado, 11/03, Lei do Fomento Empresarial, 14/03, Lei dos Incentivos Fiscais, 17/03. World Trade Organization, "Trade Policy Review: Angola, Report by the Secretariat," April 3, 2006.

well-connected local partners. At a lower level, small bribes are a part of daily life. In addition, there are concerns that "amid a partial clean-up of the oil sector, the diamond industry is growing in importance as a way of hiding private revenue flows."[13] These practices distort the economy and hinder economic development. Although Luanda's initial efforts to improve transparency in the management of oil revenue are encouraging, the Angolan government's opacity continues to impede assessment of the management of public funds, contributing to the perception of persistent corruption.

The Angolan government's response to allegations of corruption—a combination of candor, denials, and evasion—is not always helpful and increases the skepticism with which many view Angola's current efforts to promote transparency. However, a wide range of actors in Angola report that the government has taken steps to improve transparency: Angolan Finance Minister José Pedro de Morais broke precedent in 2004 by disclosing that Chevron had paid $300 million for an oil tract, a major shift from Angola's usual secrecy on financial matters. The oil-block bidding in May 2006 was the most transparent in Angola's history and an important change since 2001, when Sonangol, Angola's state-owned oil company, publicly excoriated BP for pledging to disclose financial data on Angola. In addition to signing the UN Convention against Corruption and the AU Convention on Preventing and Combating Corruption, Angola has established, with the World Bank, a program that monitors most government expenditures as they occur, and aims to monitor all expenditures by 2008. Furthermore, the climate of candor has improved in recent years—with allegations of corruption and mismanagement broached openly in the Angolan media, everyday conversations, and public meetings.

The clearest test of Angola's commitment to transparency is whether it will fully participate in the Extractive Industries Transparency Initiative (EITI). The EITI aims to support good governance in resource-rich countries through the full publication and verification of company payments and government revenues from oil, gas, and mining in both candidate and compliant countries. Angola has taken some steps to

---

[13] Chatham House, "Angola—Drivers of Change," April 2005, p. 12.

meet EITI goals by publicizing its oil revenue on the Internet (by block and revenue type) and disclosing signing bonuses in the latest bidding round of offshore oil-block bidding. But Angola has yet to meet all EITI goals and continues to forgo full participation.[14] By fully implementing EITI criteria, Angola could send a positive signal of its commitment to transparency that would influence foreign governments, the IMF, and the global private sector, thereby encouraging more international investment.

Debt Management

The IMF projected in 2005 that Angola's external debt, estimated to be $9.5 billion at the end of 2004, was sustainable in the long run, citing increased government revenue from oil production.[15] With more oil production scheduled, prospects are promising for continued economic growth and strong public finances.[16] An October 2006 World Bank report states that Angola's external debt-to-GDP ratio is expected to decline from 38.5 percent in 2005 to 34 percent in 2006, due to the expected rapid growth in GDP. In this context, the management of Angola's debt does not appear burdensome. Indeed, Angola could choose to pay off debts outright. Therefore, the issue is not necessarily debt forgiveness, but rather the terms under which Angola will pay down its debt.

Luanda is concentrating its debt management efforts on its obligations to Paris Club members. Angola is interested in paying down its $2.6 billion (2005) debt to Paris Club creditors to improve its creditworthiness, diversify its sources of financing, and obtain better rates on commercial loans. However, there cannot be a collective Paris Club agreement on a concessional repayment scheme without an IMF arrangement,

---

[14] Angola's vice minister of finance and private sector representatives participated in the EITI Oslo Conference in October 2006 as observers, indication of Angola's tentative interest in EITI.

[15] The most recent external debt figures are from 2004. The debt is public or publicly guaranteed and is a liability of either the central government or Sonangol. See IMF, "Angola: Selected Issues and Statistical Appendix," Country Report No. 05/125, April 2005, p. 41.

[16] IMF, "Angola: 2006 Article IV Consultations, Preliminary Conclusions of the IMF Mission," conclusion No. 5.

and Angola's relationship with the IMF has been uneven. The IMF's position has been that before receiving IMF support, Angola must negotiate a staff-monitored program and show a year of good performance. But the slow pace and cumbersome bureaucracy of the IMF has frustrated Angola's leadership. The government of Angola believes that the IMF has been too critical of its record on transparency, governance, macroeconomic management, and structural reform. Moreover, Angola's oil wealth and the access to international finance it provides reduces Luanda's incentives to cooperate on policy reforms.[17]

After multiple rounds of consultations, in February 2007 Angola announced that it would no longer seek to conclude an IMF agreement. Angola will, however, continue to work with the IMF on technical assistance, an indication that Luanda remains interested in strengthening its relationship with the IMF, if only because this could eventually lead to receiving Paris Club imprimatur. One future arrangement option outside the staff-monitored program framework is a Policy Support Instrument (PSI), a voluntary, IMF-guided economic reform program, designed for low-income countries that may not need or want IMF financial assistance, but would like IMF advice, monitoring, and endorsement of their policies. For this option to work, Angola's leaders must design a reform program that is acceptable to the IMF. Nigeria was able to do this, persuading the IMF to monitor a self-designed reform program, which led to a Paris Club buy-down of Nigerian debt.[18]

Capacity and Infrastructure

Any discussion of financial discrepancies in Angola's government records must take into account the country's lack of human and institutional capacity. Lacking a strong cadre of skilled workers even before the civil war, Angola began its postwar reconstruction far behind the starting line. In 2005, the Angolan government allocated $2.5 billion for public investment, but was capable of spending efficiently only $1.5 billion.

---

[17] The government appears to be moving away from oil-backed loans as it works toward securing better commercial rates for borrowing. See Global Witness, "Press Release: Western Banks to Give Huge New Loan to Angola in Further Blow to Transparency," September 23, 2005.

[18] In the final agreement with the Paris Club, Nigeria paid $6 billion in arrears up front, and then agreed to pay $6 billion more for a buy-down of the $31 billion balance.

Angola has limited capacity to record precisely the huge sums of oil money suddenly pouring into the country, one reason why it remains difficult to obtain accurate government statistics. It is essential that Angola develop the institutional capacity required to manage current and future revenue—a need recognized by the Angolan government.

At the same time, Angola faces an immense task in rebuilding its infrastructure. For starters, traveling to the interior of the country is difficult. Roads are unusable and bridges destroyed. The inland provinces of Bié, Huambo, Huíla, Moxico, and Kuando Kubango were devastated during the conflict, and have yet to be connected to the coast through transportation and communication systems. This divide, which reflects the historic division between MPLA and UNITA strongholds, creates disparities in public and commercial services, as well as living standards. Crippled transportation networks impede the delivery of goods to the domestic, let alone global, market. Land mines— still a major problem—inadequate irrigation systems, and a dearth of equipment inhibit agricultural production, stunting the growth of a non-oil economy. Broken education and public health systems contribute to a poor quality of life throughout the country.

Meanwhile, international organizations are working to improve living standards for the people of Angola. As of August 2006, the World Bank's portfolio for Angola consists of five active projects, financed by $177 million in committed credits and grants from the International Development Association (IDA), and $104 million in grants cofinanced with other donors, such as the European Commission. The International Finance Corporation is building its investment portfolio in Angola, and the Multilateral Investment Guarantee Agency is increasingly providing guarantees for private investments there. The African Development Bank focuses on the reduction of rural poverty and creation of an environment conducive to private sector development. The UNDP in cooperation with the Angolan Ministry of Planning, is working to develop Angolan institutions, de-mine territory, promote ecomonic growth in the poorest Angolan communities, and provide universal access to basic social services.

Many oil companies maintain innovative corporate social responsibility programs in Angola and are helping build capacity and infrastructure both in the communities where they operate and beyond. While they value their close relationships with oil companies, many Angolans have expressed disappointment that these companies are not doing more. Indeed, although these companies have made important contributions, more can be done. It is in the interests of all parties that obligations and encouragement be written into contracts and legislation, and that those commitments are executed on the ground.

Members of UNITA note that Angola's capacity problem is politically convenient for the MPLA, which can offer it as an excuse for why more progress has not been made. Those who argue that a lack of capacity is an excuse could cite an example from Cabinda, a critical part of Angola's economy. In Cabinda City, where the government has made a vigorous effort to restore public services, electricity and water are running more reliably than elsewhere in Angola, raising the question of whether capacity is so large an impediment when there is political will to back it up. But while there are certainly problems of political will in Angola, the human capacity and physical infrastructure problems are real and serious. In the end, political will and capacity-building must go hand in hand.

Democratic Governance and National Elections

Angola has yet to invest in the institutions of democracy—institutions that include not only a democratic political system, where leaders are held accountable and power is equitably distributed, but also an independent judiciary, a robust civil society, and a free press. Today, the institutions of democracy are not strong. The Angolan government is highly centralized and political power is wielded by a relatively small number of senior MPLA officials, all close allies of President dos Santos. This arrangement limits the ability of minority political parties, media, and civil society to observe, much less participate in, the decision-making process. But while the transition to a more just, democratic society will be long, democratization has begun. In one hopeful step, Angola has agreed to participate in the African Peer Review Mechanism, launched in 2003 as part of NEPAD to ensure oversight on political, economic, and corporate governance.

The Angolan government has also shown a growing tolerance of dissent. With only sporadic government interference, activists can build networks for change, hold demonstrations, publish articles in the independent press (limited to Luanda), give interviews to domestic and foreign radio stations, and travel to meetings outside Angola. There are more than one hundred registered Angolan NGOs. Together with Protestant and Catholic clergy, civil society groups are working to create land tenure laws, protect human rights, increase social services, and reduce poverty. These groups shy away from an advocacy role to avoid being associated with an opposition movement, but there are deepening partnerships between NGOs and the Angolan government—with government officials participating in civil society conferences and civil society groups working with government on civic education, particularly in preparation for national elections. International NGOs also operate in Angola, including the National Democratic Institute for International Affairs, International Republican Institute, Search for Common Ground, Development Workshop, and others.

But much work remains. If Angola is to become a more robust democracy, progress will need to be made in at least two critical areas: Economic wealth needs to be distributed more evenly, as it is difficult for citizens who survive on $2 per day to participate effectively in the democratic process; and a vibrant civil society must continue to develop. Individuals and organizations active on behalf of these objectives deserve encouragement.

Angola's Council of the Republic, the political consultative body of the office of the president, has recommended that parliamentary and presidential elections be held mid-2008 and mid-2009, respectively. Whether or not parliament agrees with that election schedule, the contest will take place considerably later than the 2006 date earlier pledged by President dos Santos, widely believed to be the MPLA's candidate in the presidential contest. No one disputes that the schedule of elections should be realistic and take into account infrastructure problems, but it is important to hold incident-free elections, deemed free and fair by international observers, in the near future. Elections can both help establish popular support for national reconstruction and rehabilitation policies and persuade Angolans and international observers that a democratic future is possible. Moreover, in the long run, a more equitable distribution of political power can reinforce political stability and national reconciliation. The ongoing electoral registration process, set up in accordance with the advice of a private international consortium, has registered more than two million voters in the first two months, a good down payment on the promise of elections in 2008.

Peace and Security

While it would like to play a constructive military role in Africa, Angola is clear-eyed about its own internal security challenges and the dangers of overextension. Angola also faces huge difficulties in implementing the ambitious disarmament, demobilization, and reintegration program launched after the war to help former combatants, including local militias armed by the government during the civil war, transition into peaceful roles in Angolan society. Success in disarming communities and managing the proliferation of small arms throughout the country is critical as Angola approaches elections, inasmuch as both are potential sources of intimidation and unrest.

Angola's other major security challenges are managing transnational crime and refugee movements along its long and porous border with the tumultuous DRC and securing its territorial integrity in Cabinda. Control of Cabinda, a 2,800-square-mile oil-rich province located on the border of the DRC and the Republic of the Congo, has been disputed since the movement for Angolan independence began. The Front for the Liberation of the Enclave of Cabinda (FLEC) declared independence from Portugal on August 1, 1975, a move that was not recognized by Portugal or Angola's pro-independence factions. MPLA troops entered Cabinda in November 1975, and the Treaty of Alvor, which set the terms of Angola's independence from Portugal, states that Cabinda is an integral and inalienable part of Angola. However, the treaty was not signed by the FLEC or by other representatives from Cabinda.

Over thirty years later in August 2006, a cease-fire, general amnesty for separatist combatants, and provisions for combatant demobilization were approved by FLEC-Renovada, one faction of the original FLEC, and the Angolan government. In January 2007, five hundred former separatist fighters voluntarily integrated with the FAA. Another faction, FLEC-Armed Forces of Cabinda, continues its struggle for independence both inside and outside Cabinda.

Although Cabinda remains a potential flash point of conflict, the government appears to be making progress in increasing services and programs in the province, engaging Cabindan civil society groups, discouraging outside assistance for those supporting separatism, and stepping up negotiations with Cabindan leaders. Some in the FLEC are publicizing human rights abuses by police and troops rather than pursuing change through violence. For example, in October 2006, the Republic of Cabinda in Exile and FLEC-FAC asked for intervention by the African Commission on Human and Peoples' Rights for violation of rights under the African Charter on Human and Peoples' Rights, which Angola signed in 1990. The request was presented at the commission's secretariat in November 2006, but no resolutions on the matter were adopted.

Angola faces major challenges in its security sector, including its police and military. The FAA has a large, battle-hardened army, jet fighter and helicopter pilot corps, and long-range artillery capacities, but it is not realistic to hope that it might contribute to peace and stability operations in Africa without substantial training and reform. Total FAA manpower was approximately 140,000 in 2005, the army being by far the largest of the services with nearly 130,000 members. But despite its size, few troops are well trained or well equipped, and those who are have their hands full in Cabinda and along the DRC–Angola border. In addition, the majority of the military's budget is spent on personnel, including pensions; FAA payroll includes nearly five hundred thousand people. The ongoing need to keep demobilized soldiers employed makes downsizing and streamlining extremely difficult. The FAA faces numerous other internal challenges, including replacing and maintaining outdated and broken equipment, improving soldier training, and transitioning to a peacetime military posture.

International Relations

Like many other states, Angola aims to have multiple strategic partners. Because of its colonial past, Angola has privileged partnerships with

Portugal and Brazil, major trading partners, and close ties to Russia and Israel, which have links to Angola's defense and diamond sectors.[19] Angola has had, at times, strained relations with its Cold War adversaries, South Africa and the United States. Now, Luanda is working to develop new, pragmatic relationships, the most prominent of which is with China.

In February 2006, Angola surpassed Saudi Arabia to become the number one supplier of oil to China. China's growing role in Africa has generated wide speculation and heated argument. In addition to financing multibillion-dollar oil-backed loans for Angola, rehabilitating the Benguela railroad, and constructing a new airport, China has acquired equity positions in several oil concessions. These developments may increase China's potential influence in Angola in the coming years.[20] Talks between Sonangol and Beijing's Sinopec on the construction of a multibillion-dollar refinery in Lobito, however, collapsed in early March 2007. Apparently, Sonangol has taken over sole ownership of the project, though what this bodes for the future is unclear.[21]

From both the Angolan and Chinese perspectives, the relationship is pragmatic and strategic. Angolans receive loans at lower rates than they would from commercial banks, while the Chinese receive guaranteed oil deliveries at world market price as well as business for Chinese companies.[22] But while the relationship meets the present needs of both governments, it is possible that Angola may, at some future date, decide to balance its external relations, wary of becoming too dependent on its Asian partner.

To be sure, there are causes for concern. There is a lack of transparency about Chinese operations in Angola. Loans from Beijing are funding major infrastructure projects, directed by Chinese firms and

---

[19] "Brazil's Lula Says Brazil Keen to Maintain 'Privileged Partnership' with Angola," *BBC News*, November 4, 2003. Also see "Angola Backs a Bigger Global Role for Brazil," Agencia Brasil, May 4, 2005, http://www.brazzilmag.com/content/view/2292/53/.

[20] "Angola; China Grants Additional $2 Billion Loan," Angola Press Agency, June 22, 2006.

[21] "Angola to See $50 million Oil Investment: Sonangol," Reuters, March 8, 2007. http://www.alertnet.org/thenews/newsdesk/L08456414.htm

[22] Generally, Angola sells its oil at world market price. The structure of Brazil's credit line to Angola stipulates that, if the world market price rises above an agreed dollar amount, proceeds go to Angola. This may also be true of China's credit line, but the structure for the payment of that credit line is not disclosed, so observers cannot be certain.

staffed with Chinese labor. But what is unclear is how much money is on the table, how contracts are awarded, how many Chinese are in the country, and how many Angolans are actually employed by Chinese companies operating in Angola. Furthermore, Angola should be wary of outsourcing jobs Angolans could do themselves; importing labor may be sowing the seeds of future resentment. Nonetheless, China is making significant contributions to Angola's development by building and rebuilding roads, hospitals, schools, and sanitation systems.

Turning from east to west, Angola's relationship with the United States still seems to be marked by a residue of mistrust, some left over from the Cold War and some more recent. Angolans had hoped that their UN Security Council vote with the United States on Iraq would open the door to a closer relationship. They regret that it has not. In addition, Angolans argue that the United States sets economic and political conditions on a robust relationship, which the United States denies. On the American side, many remain skeptical of Angola's progress, even when it is real. Developing a stronger relationship requires that both the United States and Angola see each other through a clear lens.

Rethinking U.S. Strategy toward Angola

It is difficult for anyone, especially an outsider, to be certain how Angola's postconflict transition will progress, but this commission believes that something significant is occurring in Angola. The country is changing—rebuilding its territory, developing its economy, and pursuing pragmatic relationships abroad. It is time for the United States to reassess its relationship accordingly.

Current U.S. Approach

From 1975 to 1989, U.S.-Angola relations were defined by Cold War politics. When the Soviet-supported MPLA came to power and declared Angola independent in November 1975, the United States opposed Angolan membership to the United Nations, fighting it until December 1976. The United States generally supported the opponents of the MPLA in Angola, at first Holden Roberto's FNLA and then Jonas Savimbi's UNITA, withholding formal diplomatic relations with Luanda until the 1992 national elections.

Since the United States recognized the Republic of Angola in 1993, and particularly since the end of the war in 2002, U.S.-Angola relations have generally improved. Then Secretary of State Colin Powell visited Angola in 2002; President George W. Bush designated Angola eligible for tariff preferences under the African Growth and Opportunity Act

(AGOA) in 2003; President dos Santos met with President Bush during an official visit to Washington in 2004; and Angola was named one of three pilot countries under President Bush's Malaria Initiative in 2006.

The U.S. Embassy in Angola, one of the United States' larger missions in southern Africa, includes representatives of the Departments of State and Defense, and the Centers for Disease Control and Prevention. The U.S. Agency for International Development (USAID), with a budget of just over $30 million in 2006, is helping on a variety of fronts, from improving food security to assisting with economic reform. Relationships with the Angolan government are also maintained by a variety of other U.S. departments and agencies, including the Departments of Transportation, Commerce, and Energy, and the Federal Aviation Administration.

America's military partnership with Angola is limited but notable. Angola recently received the first U.S. Navy ship visit in more than thirty years, and General William E. Ward, deputy commander of U.S. European Command, traveled to Luanda on a tour of southern Africa in October 2006. The U.S. Navy's work with Angola is part of a larger strategy to enhance maritime security in the Gulf of Guinea. The IMET program, which operated with a budget of under $400,000 in 2006, provides English-language training to the FAA and professional training to law enforcement officers. The Department of State's Office of Weapons Removal and Abatement is supporting continued de-mining efforts by NGOs and the Angolan government, and promoting safe access to polling places for the national election. Perhaps the most significant area of military-to-military collaboration is a joint HIV/AIDS initiative to prevent the transmission of HIV in the FAA, a collaboration valued by the Angolan government.

To an extent, the U.S. government's programmatic approach toward Angola is effective. Washington maintains a working relationship with Luanda and supports a variety of helpful projects in Angola. What has been lacking, however, is a process for building a stronger strategic relationship with Angola that would help Angola realize its full potential, both domestically and on the African continent. Such a process would also serve U.S. interests in building both a more stable region and a reliable energy partnership with one of Africa's major suppliers. The U.S.

government will always focus its attention on those African countries wracked by crisis. But among those African countries not in crisis, Angola should receive diplomatic attention and resources commensurate with its growing importance to U.S. interests and to peace and stability on the African continent.

Moving Forward

The United States must adopt a strategic vision for its relations with Angola. Developing this vision involves recognizing that Angola's importance goes beyond the profits it yields for U.S. commercial interests. Angola has the potential to become a partner that can help reinforce security and stability in Africa. Whether Angola becomes such a partner depends, in part, on whether Angolans and Americans can build a stronger relationship—and a stronger relationship requires sustained U.S. diplomatic attention and strategic resource allocation. Further steps can be taken to reach that goal, many of which are spelled out in the next section.

The tone of the U.S. approach will affect the strength of the relationship. The United States should praise what is right, but not overlook what is wrong, encouraging Angola to take those steps on democratization, transparency, and the economy that will open the door to a deeper, mutually beneficial partnership.

The United States must also recognize that engagement with Angola is a long-term proposition. Change in Angola and in U.S.-Angola relations will be generational, a point reinforced by Angola's demographics: Roughly 60 percent of its population is under age twenty.[23] The next generation is the best hope for Angola's future. Although poverty and illiteracy grip all but a fortunate few, young Angolans today have opportunities that were beyond the grasp of their parents and grandparents. Less scarred by war, they are, perhaps, more open to the possibilities of peace. With fewer memories of the sour history

---

[23] This data point is from 2004, the most recent year for which information is available. "Angola: Millennium Goals Report Summary 2005," Government of the Republic of Angola and UNDP, p. 6.

of U.S.-Angola relations, the next generation may be less skeptical of the benefits of a cooperative relationship with the United States.

A new U.S. approach, guided by committed realism—committed to helping Angola fulfill its promise, but realistic about the challenges involved—should incorporate bilateral, multilateral, and private sector strategies.

U.S. Bilateral Strategy

Large steps are not required for strengthening U.S.-Angola relations. A number of small measures would advance relations and help Angola develop. To begin, the United States can associate itself with sensible Angolan priorities, taking steps to advance shared, nonpolitical objectives, and commence regular bilateral discussion with a comprehensive agenda.

Human and institutional capacity building is a critical area in which there is convergence of what Angola wants and what the United States can help provide. Neither China nor any other country is significantly helping Angola meet its massive need for an educated and diversely skilled workforce, and the United States maintains a comparative advantage in the field of advanced education and training. Capacity-building assistance helps the United States maintain an entry point for serious dialogue with the Angolan government and indicates U.S. interest in helping Angola address its immense needs. The Department of State and USAID should seize the opportunity to build on its training initiatives, such as the Development Training Program for Portuguese-Speaking Africa.

U.S. bilateral assistance to Angola through USAID has steadily declined since 2004, primarily due to a reduction in food aid to the country. As Angola's status changes from a postconflict to a developing country—and as the Department of State and USAID undergo reorganization—it is imperative that the combined State Department-USAID annual aid not fall below $35 million, the approximate amount of U.S. bilateral assistance anticipated for 2008. The United States should continue the current practice of supplementing the funding of assistance programs by agreements with private enterprises active in Angola.[24]

---

[24] In 2006, public-private partnerships in Angola increased the bilateral assistance budget by 20 percent. For example, in March 2007 the U.S. Embassy-Luanda launched an Agricultural

The important work of NGOs in Angola depends in part on the existence of USAID grants. With that continued assistance, organizations such as Catholic Relief Services and Africare can increase efforts to rehabilitate demobilized soldiers and displaced populations, eradicate polio, prevent and treat malaria, and redevelop Angola's agricultural production. Similarly, the Africa-America Institute and other organizations can continue to augment the number of advanced education and training opportunities for Angolans in fields such as finance and engineering, to help build business and public administration programs at Angolan universities, and to train Angolan finance ministry officials in statistics, data collection and analysis, public expenditure tracking, and the English language.

Expanding technical assistance programs through other U.S. departments and agencies is also needed. U.S. Department of Treasury assistance could help the National Bank of Angola to implement effective banking regulatory structures and monetary policy. Technical assistance by the U.S. Department of Commerce could help reduce the number of bureaucratic steps necessary to conduct business in Angola, thereby attracting much-needed foreign investment outside the oil sector. In addition, the U.S. government could build on the agricultural development efforts of the University of Georgia, which recently hosted a visit by eight African ministers of agriculture, including Angola's.[25] These steps could strengthen relations between Angola and the United States, cultivate American and Angolan constituencies that support a closer relationship, and enhance Angola's ability to care for its own people.

Assisting the development of Angola's public health systems and preventing large-scale epidemics of HIV and other diseases, such as Marburg virus and cholera, are more shared objectives. Information about HIV prevalence in Angola is still scarce and surveillance expanded only recently (data are now being collected at clinics in all eighteen provinces). But while international organizations have found that HIV/AIDS prevalence rates are lower in Angola than elsewhere in the region,

---

Development and Finance Program, a five-year $5.5 million public-private partnership between USAID and Chevron Corporation.

[25] See Brad Haire, "African Group Tours UGA, Agricultural Facilities," *University of Georgia News Service*, May 5, 2005, http://www.uga.edu/news/artman/publish/050505african delegation.shtml.

largely as a result of Angola's isolation during the war, vigilance is required to prevent a major epidemic that could devastate Angola's economy and society.[26] The concern is real: Lack of health care, significantly young and mobile populations, and lack of education all contribute to the potential for a larger epidemic.

The United States, through IMET programs, can also assist in the development of a professional Angolan military by helping the FAA improve efficiency and address its internal challenges. Military-to-military cooperation through the new U.S. Africa Command could build upon ongoing security cooperation efforts and create new opportunities to strengthen the capabilities of the FAA to become a partner in peace and stability operations, if Angola is willing to participate in such operations. The United States can also collaborate with the FAA in the international effort to reconstitute and professionalize the DRC's military. Before the United States can develop a closer military collaboration with Angola, however, Washington must develop a deeper political understanding of Angola's military objectives through dialogue.

Regarding civil security, expanding the training of Angolan law enforcement officials through the ILEA in Gaborone, Botswana, can improve police professionalism and help the United States and Angola cooperate on combating transnational crime. The same goals will be served by working with Angola to build a police institution development program tailored to Angola's particular needs—the specialty of the U.S. Department of Justice's ICITAP.

This discussion, however, raises concerns about whether it is necessary or appropriate to offer bilateral assistance to an oil-rich country—particularly one that has not fulfilled IMF requirements for transparency in oil accounts. The bilateral assistance this commission recommends, however, is important and targeted, focused on the development of institutions and human capital. Over time, the terms, conditions, and payment of this assistance can be negotiated among the U.S. and Angolan governments, private sector, and NGO communities, with

---

[26] According to the World Health Organization and the Joint United Nations Programme on HIV/AIDS, HIV prevalence in Angola is estimated to be less than 5 percent, compared with over 25 percent in Botswana, Lesotho, and Swaziland, and with 10 to 25 percent in nearly every other country in the region. See "AIDS Epidemic Update: December 2005," pp. 20–25.

the U.S. government sometimes serving as facilitator and sometimes as a funder. At the same time, this assistance must not undermine the IMF's reform efforts in Angola. The United States, however, should not forgo providing Angola with bilateral assistance, particularly technical assistance, that serves fundamental U.S. interests in helping build a more responsive government, a stronger rule of law, and a more favorable investment climate in Angola.

A stronger relationship should also be cultivated through a wide-ranging discussion of economic, political, and security issues specific to Angola, including banking regulation, monetary policy, access to credit, democratic development, human rights, and reforms in the energy sector, especially electricity distribution. Bilateral discussions should also include larger regional concerns, such as small arms trafficking, HIV/AIDS, and economic integration. Such a dialogue offers an opportunity to establish mutual understanding, build trust, and discuss those gestures that the pragmatic Angolans view as the mark of a strong partner. Consultations with the Angolan government on subregional issues can give U.S. policymakers additional perspectives on developments in the DRC, Zimbabwe, and Mozambique, and ideas about how China and the United States can cooperate on development and security in Africa.

Finally, the individuals and organizations in and outside of Angola striving to create a democratic country, where good governance and sharing an equitable distribution of national wealth are regarded as national priorities, deserve encouragement. As part of this encouragement, the United States should continue to engage with courageous civil society leaders, journalists, and other community activists who represent the demand side of governance.

U.S. Multilateral Strategy

Engaging Angola through multilateral settings can complement and enhance U.S.-Angola bilateral relations. But when utilizing multilateral channels to advance the goals of regional security, stability, and development, it would be unwise and inaccurate for the United States to view Angola's other partners as adversaries. Angola and those states and businesses invested in its future share many of the same interests. No one wants to see Angola fail or fall back into conflict. Few would prefer corruption to transparency. Most want to see Angola develop its capacity, rebuild its infrastructure, and improve its regulatory environment so that it attracts global business. Most prefer a more democratic future, which, over the long run, means a more stable future. There is, to some extent, consensus on these broader aims, and the United States should work with Angola and its partners to advance a collective agenda.

One option for multilateral engagement is the SADC-U.S. Forum. The forum, established in 1999, meets annually to discuss the political and security situation in the region, and to evaluate progress in areas of cooperation. The United States could propose that the next meeting be held in Luanda, and that the forum's political roundtable discussions focus on postconflict developments in Angola and the DRC.

Another setting is the AU. With fifty-three member states, the AU is Africa's principal organization for the promotion of peace and security, democratic principles, and good governance, and for the protection of human rights in accordance with the African charter. It is important that the United States support the AU in this challenging and worthwhile endeavor, both behind the scenes and publicly, particularly as it relates to Angola.

The U.S. government should engage Angola in multilateral settings and in coordination with international institutions, while being realistic about its ability to influence change in Angola through U.S. involvement in international financial institutions, which have a mixed record of promoting reforms in developing countries in Africa.

One possibility, originally recommended by the official representatives of donor countries in Luanda, is an international investment conference on Angola. Without requiring financial commitments like a donor conference, this gathering would be an opportunity for Angolan government and international stakeholders to discuss how to strengthen partnerships, prioritize development goals, and build the capacity Angola needs for sustained growth.

In addition to the World Bank's IDA, the principal multilateral channel for U.S. aid, the United States can contribute more to the African Development Bank and UNDP's activities in Africa. The Norwegian Ministry of Foreign Affairs signed an $800,000 cost-sharing agreement for a civic education program with UNDP. In December

2006, Japan gave approximately $4 million to Angola through UNDP to strengthen the technical and operational capacity of the National Institute for Demining in Angola. The United States should consider similar contributions to multilateral efforts in support of specific capacity challenges.

In addition, the United States can offer technical assistance to facilitate a productive relationship between Angola and the IMF, but the details of that relationship should be decided by the two parties.

Private Sector Strategy

A new U.S.-Angola approach must also include a role for the private sector. Angola is highly aware of the lack of U.S. private investment (outside the oil sector), which reflects the inhospitable investment climate. In truth, greater levels of U.S. private sector investment in Angola depend more on action by the Angolan government than by the U.S. government. Investment will increase when the Angolan government takes steps to make its business climate more user-friendly and its overall economy less dependent on oil. Foreign consultants can recommend ways to do this, but the decision to improve the investment climate rests with the Angolans.

That said, there are a number of strategies the U.S. government can pursue to complement the work currently undertaken by the Angolan government, the U.S.-Angola Chamber of Commerce, the Corporate Council on Africa, and other nonprofits that are building bridges to Angolan business. These strategies include trade and investment missions, launched by U.S. government departments and conducted by financiers and businesspeople in a range of sectors, with the goal of expanding commercial ties.

As their dialogue deepens, the United States and Angola should look for ways to diversify Angola's economy and increase trade. Angola is currently a beneficiary of AGOA, but its main export is oil. As opportunities for wider investments develop, the United States should put on the table the prospect of a free trade agreement with Angola. An FTA would not be immediately beneficial but could be a building block for a broader, long-term trade relationship. Putting forward the idea would also signal recognition of Angola's importance to the United

States. Pursuing a bilateral investment treaty is another option, but would require some preliminary steps by the Angolan government, such as adhering to the convention on mandatory arbitration. A near-term goal would be to conclude a TIFA between the two governments.

The private sector also has an important role to play in meeting Angola's capacity needs. In fact, while its experience with external involvement is not always viewed favorably, the Angolan government has been willing to privatize and outsource to private firms. In recent years, private firms have managed Luanda's port terminals and garbage collection system, and the Ministry of Finance has used foreign consultants to help build its financial programming capacity. Oil companies and other businesses can provide more scholarships for Angolan students. In the long run, however, Angola must become self-sufficient, capable of meeting its capacity needs on its own.

U.S. Policy Recommendations

To help Angola and the United States meet their evolving needs, the commission recommends a combination of U.S. bilateral, multilateral, and private sector strategies. To be effective, the United States must be prepared to make a long-term commitment and structure its short-term policies in a way that facilitates lasting change in Angola.

U.S. Bilateral Approach

As made clear in this report, many elements of a sound U.S. policy toward Angola are already in place. The United States has a significant and talented diplomatic mission on the ground in Luanda, managing programs to help Angola address its most vital issues. But, as is the case in any bilateral relationship, the U.S. approach can be strengthened with careful consideration of fresh initiatives.

However, the issue is less U.S. policy content than the priority that the U.S. government currently assigns to the Angola relationship. This report argues that Angola should be treated on a par with the continent's leading states. From this commitment, the rest follows: regular high-level political, security, and economic dialogue; sharp focus on political, transparency, rule of law, and economic developments in Angola; careful consideration of the external debt that clouds Angola's future; priority attention to investment and trade; and enhanced military-to-military cooperation. To put it another way, the programmatic recommendations in this report are secondary. Most important is our strategic recommendation: The commission calls upon the most senior levels of the U.S. government to recognize Angola's growing importance to U.S. interests and act accordingly.

To articulate and execute a U.S. policy that accords priority to building a strong relationship with Angola, an assignment of responsibility within the U.S. government must be clear, and a mechanism for regular bilateral dialogue must be established. These do not exist today to the degree required, but are necessary in order to bring focus to the U.S.-Angola relationship.

It may not be practical to establish a high-level bilateral commission to improve the dialogue with Angola because the Bush administration has shunned such arrangements. Nevertheless, the U.S. president should inform the Angolan government of the importance the United States places on an improved and regular dialogue, adding that the secretary of state and assistant secretary of state for African affairs will be charged with establishing a mechanism for this dialogue. This mechanism can include regular talks in Angola on an agreed agenda of issues and areas of mutual interest—from transparency and a timetable for elections to regional security and the aims and abilities of the FAA. It could also involve visits by Angolan ministers to the United States to meet with their American counterparts and develop further means of cooperation. The secretary of state can empower this dialogue by making clear that the results will be communicated regularly to the secretary's office and form part of the high-level dialogue that takes place among the secretary, the president, and, on the other side, the most senior officials of the Angolan government. The U.S. ambassador to Angola is responsible for organizing its execution, but ultimately responsibility for the success of Angola policy within the U.S. government lies at higher levels in Washington.

While developing a partnership with Angola, the United States should communicate with China on mutual interests in Africa. China may not be a strong supporter of democracy in Africa, but good governance, stability, and equitable growth on the continent are as much in China's interests as they are in the United States' interests. The Department of State began a dialogue with China on Africa, but it has not developed very far. This dialogue should continue and its agenda should grow to include issues of governance, transparency, corporate responsibility, and environmental degradation as they relate to Angola and other African countries where China plays an active role.

Additionally, the commission recommends:

- The Bush administration launch a series of visits by congressional delegations and high-level administration officials, such as the undersecretary of state for economic affairs, to southern African states, including Angola, that are making progress in democratic and economic development. These visits must be part of a strategy to establish and sustain dialogue over economic policy, foreign affairs, and regional security.

- The assistant secretary of state for African affairs visit Luanda to discuss Angola's national elections, capacity needs, and postconflict reconstruction and reconciliation process, as well as to compare assessments about developments in the DRC and Zimbabwe.

- The U.S. Department of State invite mid- and senior-level Angolan officials to participate in the International Visitor Leadership Program and other exchange initiatives designed to cultivate links with the current and future leadership of foreign countries.

- The U.S. Department of State facilitate a discussion with the Angolan government and representatives of the U.S. private sector, nonprofit community, and higher education to explore the possibility of public-private partnerships in capacity building and technical assistance.

- The U.S. government maintain the approximately $35 million of U.S. bilateral assistance to Angolan institutions currently anticipated for 2008. Such funds should continue to provide technical assistance for democratic institution building, civil society, education and professional training, financial and land reform, agricultural development, and public health. Specifically, the Department of State's nonproliferation, antiterrorism, de-mining, and related programs funding, which supports the development of Angola's de-mining capability and the management and destruction of small arms, should not fall below the current $6 million for the next five years. Funding for IMET programs aimed at developing apolitical and transparent defense institutions, such as training in civil-military relations, defense budgeting, and human rights, should be increased to $600,000.

- The U.S. Embassy should discuss with Angola the possibility of expanding current law-enforcement training programs with the ILEA and establishing police institutional development programs through ICITAP. Programming should include community policing, election security and civil disturbance techniques, and academy development.

- The U.S. Department of Defense make building rapport with Angola a priority of the new U.S. Africa Command. Increased engagement with the FAA, through contacts and briefings with FAA leadership, should focus on the progress of disarmament, demobilization, and reintegration of former combatants; developments in the DRC; and the role of the FAA in postconflict Angola. Furthermore, the Department's Africa Center for Strategic Studies initiative can work to hold some of its leadership and topical seminars in Angola.

- The U.S. Department of Education launch an initiative of U.S. university presidents to assess the feasibility of educational exchanges and institutional partnerships with Angolan universities.

- The U.S. Department of State deepen initiatives to engage China regarding shared interests in Africa.

U.S. Multilateral Approach

While this commission concludes that building on the already good U.S.-Angola bilateral relations should be a higher priority than multilateral relations, it is important to ensure that Angola continues to integrate into global markets and regional organizations and resolves its external debts.

The commission recommends that:

- The United States propose holding a SADC-U.S. Forum summit meeting in Luanda.

- The United States support an international investment and economic development conference for Angola, as recommended by the official representatives of donor countries in Luanda. This conference would be an opportunity for Angolan government and development stakeholders to discuss how to strengthen partnerships, prioritize development goals, and build the capacity Angola needs for sustained growth.

- The United States prepare to offer a technical assistance package that complements any future cooperation between Angola and the IMF.

The Promotion of Private Sector Relationships

To develop international private sector relationships in Angola, thereby complementing efforts by the Angolan government to create a better investment climate, the commission recommends that:

- The United States articulate an FTA as a goal toward which the U.S. and Angolan governments can aspire, and set milestones for its completion, including an agreement on a TIFA to establish a consultative mechanism between the U.S. trade representative and the Angolan government.

- The United States continue the current practice of supplementing the funding for bilateral assistance programs by public-private agreements with private enterprises active in Angola.

- The U.S. Department of Commerce launch trade and investment missions, particularly for agricultural and agribusiness companies, and establish a permanent presence in the U.S. mission in Angola.

- American businesses operating in Angola, particularly oil companies, expand support for Angolan education institutions and support more advanced education and training opportunities for Angolan students.

Conclusion

This report is being issued at a time when recent spikes in the price of oil and U.S. oil dependency have refocused America's attention toward relationships with energy-producing states. With few exceptions, countries upon which the United States depends for its energy supplies are either in politically unstable regions of the world or rank poorly in terms of human development and governance. This poses significant strategic and political challenges for U.S. policymakers, given that the United States has a long history of promoting democratic governance and values, believing that democratic states make better long-term bilateral partners and contribute to international stability. Angola is one such country that poses an awkward policy dilemma for the United States.

This commission believes that U.S. strategic interests in energy and security in the Gulf of Guinea would be served by strengthening the ties between the United States and Angola as part of a broad energy policy and a strategic approach toward Africa. An integral part of this policy must also be for the United States to support those individuals in Angola—political leaders, community activists, and civil society leaders—who are striving to create a democratic country where good governance and sharing an equitable distribution of national wealth are regarded as national priorities. Angola's progress in these critical areas goes hand in hand with building a stronger bilateral relationship between the United States and Angola as recommended by the commission.

Furthermore, the policy that the United States adopts toward Angola should recognize Angola's role in the global energy market, but be tailored to helping Angola address its particular situation. Creating a more equitable society in which Angola's leaders are politically accountable is the best long-run conflict prevention policy.

Real reform and equitable development, of course, cannot be imposed from outside. Fortunately, with Angola's oil wealth, both goals are realistic if Luanda makes the right choices at home and abroad. This report shows that there are some specific steps the Angolan government could take that would be welcomed by the country's international political and economic partners, and would provide a stronger foundation on which to build and deepen bilateral relations between the United States and Angola. These include setting a specific date to hold elections and starting to put in place the necessary structures to ensure that the election is free and fair. In order to gain the respect it desires internationally, the Angolan government must become more accountable to its people. Having democratic elections would be an important step in the process.

Other actions the Angolan government could take that would have a favorable impact abroad include becoming a full participant in the EITI and simplifying the approval process for foreign investments in Angola. Such investments, especially beyond the oil and diamond sectors, could stimulate economic activity, diversify the economy, and create much-needed jobs. This means becoming considerably more user-friendly to foreign investors. If this were to happen, the commission believes that U.S. private sector investment in Angola would increase significantly from the current low level.

Wide-ranging bilateral dialogue between Angola and the United States can help achieve progress toward common objectives. By working in partnership with international and regional organizations like the UN, World Bank, and AU, the United States can support and encourage those individuals and institutions in Angola who want to seize this moment to build Angolan capacity and move the country on a path to a more democratic and transparent society. This can be done without undermining in any way the development of a stronger bilateral partnership between the United States and Angola. Indeed, by articulating clearly and consistently its faith in democracy and the rule of law, the United States can play a helpful role as a partner to Angola as the

Angolans themselves take the lead in using their abundance of human and natural resources to create a more democratic society, committed to human rights and sustainable economic development.

While the path ahead will be long and difficult, a successful relationship will help both the United States and Angola build a better future—and that is a goal worth striving for.

Commission Members

Kofi Appenteng is a partner at Thacher Proffitt & Wood LLP. Mr. Appenteng is active in many professional and civic organizations, including the Africa-America Institute, where he serves as board chair; the Community Service Society of New York; the Institute for International and Comparative Law; Instituto de Empresa; University of Cape Town Fund, Inc.; the Association of the Bar of the City of New York; and the New York State Bar Association.

Peter W. Baird is group president for therapeutic devices at Encore Medical Corporation. Previously, he was a partner in McKinsey & Company's Mid-Atlantic Office. Prior to joining McKinsey, Mr. Baird was a principal at Brait Capital Partners Ltd., a South African private equity firm, and he was an economics lecturer at the University of Cape Town. He also worked as an investment banker at Lehman Brothers in New York.

Pauline H. Baker is president of the Fund for Peace, a research and educational organization that works to prevent war and alleviate the conditions that cause war. A political scientist who lived in sub-Saharan Africa for over a decade and traveled throughout the continent, Baker has taught at the University of Lagos in Nigeria, the Johns Hopkins School of Advanced International Studies, and Georgetown University's Edmund A. Walsh School of Foreign Service. She was also a professional staff member of the Senate Foreign Relations Committee and staff director of the African Affairs Subcommittee. She has published over eighty articles, essays, and books, and is one of the coauthors of the *Failed States Index*, the first global ranking of conflict risk within states.

Malik M. Chaka is the director of threshold countries for the Millennium Challenge Corporation. He served as a professional staff member with the Africa Subcommittee of the House International Relations Committee for seven years. Mr. Chaka has followed developments in Angola for more than three decades and has traveled widely in the country. He testified before Congress on Angola in 1994. He has written on Angola topics in the *Times of Zambia*, *Zambia Daily Mail*, London-based *Africa Analysis*, and *Terra Angolana*, and edits an internationally distributed Angola Listserv.

Herman J. Cohen is a retired U.S. diplomat. His most senior positions were ambassador to Senegal, Africa director in the National Security Council, and assistant secretary of state for African Affairs under President George H.W. Bush. He now lectures at Johns Hopkins University and consults for U.S. businesses in Africa.

Julius E. Coles is the president of Africare. Before assuming this position, he was the director of Morehouse College's Andrew Young Center for International Affairs from 1997 to 2002. He served as the director of Howard University's Ralph J. Bunche International Affairs Center from 1994 to 1997. Mr. Coles retired from the U.S. Foreign Service in 1994 with the rank of career minister. Most of Mr. Coles's career of some twenty-eight years in the U.S. Foreign Service was spent as a senior official with USAID. He was mission director in Swaziland and Senegal and served in Vietnam, Morocco, Liberia, Nepal, and Washington, DC.

Chester A. Crocker is the James R. Schlesinger Professor of Strategic Studies at Georgetown University's Walsh School of Foreign Service. He served as chairman of the board of the United States Institute of Peace from 1992 to 2004, and continues as a member of its board. From 1981 to 1989, he was U.S. assistant secretary of state for African affairs and mediated the prolonged negotiations among Angola, Cuba, and South Africa that led to Namibia's transition to independence, and to the withdrawal of Cuban forces from Angola. He serves as a member of the boards of various public and private companies and not-for-profit institutions. Dr. Crocker is the author of *High Noon in Southern Africa: Making Peace in a Rough Neighborhood,* coauthor (with Fen Osler Hampson and Pamela Aall) of *Taming Intractable Conflicts: Mediation in the Hardest Cases,* and coeditor (with Fen Osler Hampson and Pamela Aall) of *Grasping the Nettle: Analyzing Cases of Intractable Conflict.*

Frank E. Ferrari is president of ProVentures Inc., an international advisory group with a major focus on Africa. He was formerly acting president and senior vice president of the Africa-America Institute, heading up its office in South Africa from 1992 to 1994. He is a member of the South North Development Initiative, and the African adviser to the International Advisory Board of Independent Newspapers. He is a graduate of New York University, and former member of the Africa Faculty Seminar at Columbia University.

Adam P. Frankel was a Rosenthal Fellow in the Office of the Coordinator for Counterterrorism at the U.S. Department of State and has worked in the Office of Presidential Speechwriting at the White House. He was educated at Princeton University and the London School of Economics and Political Science, where he was a Fulbright scholar.

David L. Goldwyn is president of Goldwyn International Strategies, LLC. He served previously as assistant secretary of energy for international affairs (1999–2001) and counselor to the secretary of energy (1998–99), working on international energy policy, international science and technology policy, international oil emergencies, and trade and investment issues. He was senior adviser and counsel to the U.S. Ambassador to the UN (1997–98). He has also served in the U.S. Department of State as chief of staff to the undersecretary for political affairs (1993–97), special assistant to undersecretaries Arnold Kanter and Peter Tarnoff (1992–93), and attorney in the Office of the Legal Adviser (1991–92).

Paul J. Hare is executive director of the U.S.-Angola Chamber of Commerce. A career officer of the U.S. Foreign Service, he served as ambassador to Zambia from 1985 to 1988 and U.S. special representative for the Angolan peace process from 1993 to 1998. He is the author of *Angola's Last Best Chance for Peace: An Insider's Account of the Peace Process.*

Patrick Hayford is the director of the UN Office of the special adviser for Africa.

Edward V.K. Jaycox is a managing director of Emerging Markets Partnership Global, a private equity investment firm, and the chief executive officer of the AIG African Infrastructure Fund. Mr. Jaycox is chairman of the boards of the West Africa Growth Fund and the Central Africa Growth Fund. He was an officer of the World Bank for over thirty years and the longest-serving regional vice president for Africa (1984–1996).

Princeton N. Lyman is the adjunct senior fellow for Africa policy studies at the Council on Foreign Relations. He is also adjunct professor at Georgetown University. From 1999 to 2003, he was executive director of the Global Interdependence Initiative at the Aspen Institute. Before that, he worked with the U.S. government, serving as deputy assistant secretary of state for African Affairs, ambassador to Nigeria, director of refugee programs, ambassador to South Africa, assistant secretary of state for international organization affairs, and director of USAID in Ethiopia. Ambassador Lyman is a member of several boards, including the American Academy of Diplomacy, the Fund for Peace, Childreach/Plan, the Amy Biehl Foundation, and the U.S.-South Africa Business Council. He also cochairs the Southern Africa Working Group for the Corporate Council on Africa.

Callisto Madavo is a visiting professor to the African Studies Program at Georgetown University. Previously, he held several senior-level positions in the World Bank, including regional vice president for the Africa region, country director for East Asia, country director for East Africa, as well as division chief of the Pakistan Programs department.

Most recently, he served as a special adviser to the president of the World Bank.

Vincent A. Mai is chairman of AEA Investors LLC, a global private equity firm with offices in the United States, Europe, and Asia. Prior to joining AEA in 1989, he was a managing director of Lehman Brothers, where he was cohead of investment banking. He has served on the boards of several institutions, including the Council on Foreign Relation and the Carnegie Corporation of New York. He is chairman of the board of Sesame Workshop and also serves on the boards of the Juilliard School and the International Center for Transitional Justice. Mr. Mai is the chairman of the Africa Policy Studies Advisory Board at the Council on Foreign Relations and chairman of the Africa Advisory Committee at Human Rights Watch.

Mora L. McLean is president and chief executive officer of the Africa-America Institute (AAI), the oldest U.S.-based nonprofit organization concerned with promoting U.S.-Africa relations through education, training, and dialogue. She joined AAI from the Ford Foundation, where she was deputy director for Africa and Middle East Programs and before that, the West Africa representative based in Lagos, Nigeria. She is a Wesleyan University trustee and member of New York University's adjunct faculty. She also serves on the boards of directors of the U.S. Institute of Peace in Washington, DC, and the U.S. International University in Nairobi, Kenya; the Advisory Board of the Management Education and Research Consortium; and the Advisory Commission for the Abraham Lincoln Study Abroad Fellowship Program established by Congress.

M. Peter McPherson is president of the National Association of State Universities and Land-Grant Colleges and president emeritus of Michigan State University (1993–2004). From April to October 2003, he took leave from Michigan State and served as the director of economic policy in Iraq under the Coalition Provisional Authority. Prior to that, Mr. McPherson held senior executive positions with the Bank of

America (1989–93) and the U.S. government, including deputy secretary of treasury (1987–89), administrator of USAID (1981–87), and special assistant to President Gerald R. Ford. He chairs the board of the Commission on the Abraham Lincoln Study Abroad Fellowship Program, is the founding cochair of the Partnership to Cut Hunger and Poverty in Africa, is chairman of the Board for International Food and Agricultural Development, and serves on the board of directors of Dow Jones & Company, Inc.

William L. Nash is the General John W. Vessey senior fellow for conflict prevention and director of the Center for Preventive Action at the Council on Foreign Relations. Major General Nash (U.S. Army, Ret.) has extensive experience in peacekeeping operations, both as a military commander in Bosnia-Herzegovina and as a civilian administrator for the UN in Kosovo. After serving in the Army for thirty-four years, he has been a fellow and visiting lecturer at Harvard's John F. Kennedy School of Government and director of Civil-Military Programs at the National Democratic Institute for International Affairs. In addition to his duties at the Council, he is also a professorial lecturer at Georgetown University, a visiting lecturer at Princeton University, and a military consultant to ABC News.

Arthur Mark Rubin is the head of Morgan Stanley's liability management group, based in New York. He previously held positions with Goldman Sachs, ABN AMRO, and Bankers Trust in New York and Sao Paulo, Brazil. He has been involved in debt restructuring and liability management transactions for a variety of corporate and sovereign borrowers, including Brazil, Mexico, Argentina, Colombia, Venezuela, and Uruguay. Prior to his career in finance, Mr. Rubin served as the executive director of the U.S.-Angola Chamber of Commerce. Mr. Rubin received his BA from Yale University, BA (Honors) from the University of Cape Town, and his MA in International Relations and African Studies from the Paul H. Nitze School of Advanced International Studies at Johns Hopkins University.

Marian L. Tupy is a policy analyst with the Cato Institute's Center for Global Liberty and Prosperity, specializing in the study of Europe and sub-Saharan Africa. His articles have been published in, among others, the *Financial Times* and *Wall Street Journal Europe*. He received his BA in international relations and classics from the University of the Witwatersrand in Johannesburg, South Africa, and received his PhD in international relations from the University of St. Andrews in Great Britain.

Nancy J. Walker is president of AfricaNet, an independent international institute focusing on human security and security sector governance in Africa and serving as a professional development resource to civilian, military, and civil society leaders throughout the continent. In early 2004, Dr. Walker resigned from U.S. government service after almost fifteen years. She also works with the UN Office for West Africa, the UN Office of the Special Adviser on Africa, the International Peace Academy, Femmes Africa Solidarité, and other organizations. She serves on the international advisory board of the Geneva Center for the Democratic Control of the Armed Forces and on the board of directors of the U.S. Committee for the United Nations Development Programme.

Steven D. Winch is a vice president at Ripplewood Holdings LLC, a New York-based private equity fund, where he has invested in both domestic and emerging markets. Previously, he worked at McKinsey & Company, Inc. on assignments across the United States, Asia, Australia, Latin America, and Eastern Europe. Prior to McKinsey, he worked in mergers and acquisitions at Salomon Brothers Inc.

Frank G. Wisner is vice chairman of external affairs at American International Group, Inc. A career diplomat with the personal rank of career ambassador, the highest grade in the senior Foreign Service, he served as U.S. ambassador to India (1994–97). Additionally, he was ambassador to Zambia (1979–82), Egypt (1986–91), and the Philippines (1991–92). Ambassador Wisner has served in a number of senior positions in the U.S. government, including undersecretary of defense for policy (1993–94), undersecretary of state for international security affairs (1992–93), senior deputy assistant secretary for African affairs (1982–86), director of the Office of Southern African Affairs (1976), and deputy executive secretary of the Department of State (1977).

James D. Zirin is a member of Sidley Austin LLP, where he is a partner in the litigation department. He was formerly an assistant U.S. attorney for the southern district of New York under Robert M. Morgenthau. He has contributed hundreds of op-ed articles on legal and foreign policy subjects to the *Los Angeles Times*, the *Washington Times*, the *London Times*, and *Forbes*. He is the cohost of the cable television talk show *Digital Age*. He is a member of the advisory board of the Woodrow Wilson School of Public and International Affairs at Princeton University and a fellow of the American College of Trial Lawyers.

Mission Statement of the Center for Preventive Action

The Center for Preventive Action seeks to help prevent, defuse, or resolve deadly conflicts around the world and to expand the body of knowledge on conflict prevention. It does so by creating a forum in which representatives of governments, international organizations, nongovernmental organizations, corporations, and civil society can gather to develop operational and timely strategies for promoting peace in specific conflict situations. The center focuses on conflicts in countries or regions that affect U.S. interests but may be otherwise overlooked; where prevention appears possible; and when the resources of the Council on Foreign Relations can make a difference. The center does this by:

- *Convening Independent Preventive Action Commissions* composed of Council members, staff, and other experts. The commissions devise a practical, actionable conflict-prevention strategy tailored to the facts of the particular conflict.

- *Issuing Council Special Reports* to evaluate and respond rapidly to developing conflict situations and formulate timely, concrete policy recommendations that the U.S. government, international community, and local actors can use to limit the potential for deadly violence.

- *Engaging the U.S. government and news media* in conflict prevention efforts. The center's staff and commission members meet with administration officials and members of Congress to brief on CPA's findings and recommendations; facilitate contacts between U.S. officials and critical local and external actors; and raise awareness among journalists of potential flash points around the globe.

- *Building networks with international organizations and institutions* to complement and leverage the Council's established influence in the U.S. policy arena and increase the impact of CPA's recommendations.

- *Providing a source of expertise on conflict prevention* to include research, case studies, and lessons learned from past conflicts that policymakers and private citizens can use to prevent or mitigate future deadly conflicts.

Center for Preventive Action
Advisory Committee